UNDER PRESSURE
HOW TO AVOID GETTING SQUASHED BY STRESS

CLAIRE PEDRICK & ANDY MORGAN

By the same authors:
Friends First

Copyright © Claire Pedrick and
Andy Morgan 2004
First published 2004
ISBN 1 84427 008 4

Scripture Union, 207–209
Queensway, Bletchley,
Milton Keynes, MK2 2EB, England.
Email: info@scriptureunion.org.uk
Website:
www.scriptureunion.org.uk

Scripture Union Australia,
Locked Bag 2, Central Coast Business
Centre, NSW 2252
Website: www.su.org.au

Scripture Union USA,
PO Box 987, Valley Forge, PA 19482
Website: www.scriptureunion.org

All rights reserved. No part of this publication may be reproduced, stored in a retrieval system, or transmitted in any form or by any means, electronic, mechanical, photocopying, recording or otherwise, without the prior permission of Scripture Union.

The right of Claire Pedrick and Andy Morgan to be identified as authors of this work has been asserted by them in accordance with the Copyright, Designs and Patents Act 1988.

Unless otherwise stated, Scripture quotations are from the Contemporary English Version published by HarperCollins Publishers, copyright © 1991, 1992, 1995 American Bible Society.

Scripture marked (THE MESSAGE) copyright © Eugene H Peterson, 1993, 1994, 1995, 1996, 2000, 2001, 2002. Used by permission of NavPress Publishing Group.

Scripture marked (NIV) is taken from the Holy Bible, New International Version. Copyright © 1973, 1978, 1984 by International Bible Society. Anglicisation copyright © 1979, 1984, 1989. Used by permission of Hodder and Stoughton Limited.

British Library Cataloguing-in-Publication Data.
A catalogue record of this book is available from the British Library.

Printed and bound in Great Britain by Creative Print and Design (Wales) Ebbw Vale.

Cover: Hurlock Design
Internal design: kwgraphicdesign

Scripture Union is an international Christian charity working with churches in more than 130 countries, providing resources to bring the good news about Jesus Christ to children, young people and families and to encourage them to develop spiritually through the Bible and prayer.

As well as our network of volunteers, staff and associates who run holidays, church-based events and school Christian groups, we produce a wide range of publications and support those who use our resources through training programmes.

Acknowledgements

Thanks to all the young people who were honest with us. And there are enough of you that no one will ever know who said what! So thank you Adam, Alice, Cara, Catherine, Emily, Katherine, Kester, Kim, Kirstie, Laura, Leonette, Mark, Melissa, Michael, Oli, Rebecca, Samantha and the Letchworth Crusader Inters.

Thanks to Lucy and Ellie for going MAD while I took time out to write. And a big thank you to Samuel, who was born while we were writing this book. I hope that when you reach teenage-hood, this might be of some help to you. We love you!

contents

Note to parents	4
Intro: stress!	8

Tough stuff: dealing with loss
- Help! I can't cope! — 12
- Moving away — 14
- Piggy in the middle — 16
- I wish I were immortal — 21

Big stuff: pressures from the world we live in
- Bombs and big news — 26
- Worries about the environment — 29

"Good-enough" stuff: dealing with the pressure to succeed
- It's Monday again — 32
- Homework — 34
- SATS and exams – groan! — 38
- Time and space — 39
- Pressure from parents — 43
- Sibling rivalry — 47
- Pressure to earn money and get a job — 49
- What next? — 53
- Communication probs — 59

Rough stuff: pressure to fit in
- Body matters — 62
- PG, 12A, 15… — 68
- All my mates smoke and drink — 72

God stuff: Pressure as a Christian teen
- How do I talk about God with my friends? — 75
- The number one best-seller — 79
- Sometimes I have doubts… — 83
- Prayer pressures — 85
- Disliking people — 88
- My friend says those people in the church down the road aren't Christians — 90
- What about other religions? — 92

Index	96

Note to Parents

So yours is the only home in your area with a stressed teenager? It can feel like that sometimes. But it's not true. Young people are under an enormous amount of pressure. They have to deal with physical changes at the same time as moving schools, taking exams and living in an imperfect world where people argue, become ill and bad things happen.

In *Under Pressure* we take a look at many of the things which cause stress, exploring what the Bible says and looking at ways to cope with it.

You probably picked this up either because your teenager is under pressure, or because *you* feel under pressure with a teenager in the house! Sometimes, putting pressure on young people can be really effective. Sometimes it isn't. How do you decide when it's good? And when it's not?

Why does your teen need this book?

In *Under Pressure*, you'll find some practical ways to handle stress. Sometimes just knowing that you're not the only one who is stressed can make a huge difference.

You might both want to read this book then talk about some of the issues. If you want to avoid conflict, you could each take it in turns to describe how you feel about some of the points. No interrupting! After your teen has talked for five minutes, you could tell them what you are hearing… and then you'd have a chance to describe how you feel about the same issue, with an opportunity for your teen to give you feedback. This is a powerful way of listening, and can break the grunt/shout cycle which might be the norm in your family.

Communication

You may well be living in a house where you wake up one morning to find that your communicative and articulate child has left home and a grunting clone has moved into their bedroom! Conversations may have given way to monosyllabic noises. This may well elicit complaints from you when you don't seem to be able to communicate. And then you're accused of nagging! You want the best for your teenagers, and you are concerned for them and want to protect them. They, in turn, are quickly developing their own personalities... which won't be the same as yours!

"If we talk, it's because we want to. And if we grunt, it's because we don't. Sometimes I just might not want to talk."

Communication is the key. And it's a two-way thing. So if you get a grunt when you try to have a conversation, you could try suggesting they talk to you when they're ready.

Helping them develop into adults

As you help your children slowly develop into adults, they begin to understand that they're not the centre of the world and need to accept others. It's tough. There are loads of changes going on at school, in their bodies and in their peer groups. You are giving them more responsibility. And they may be choosing to take more, as well. Change is exciting. Change is stressful. How can you help them to mark the changes?

"Don't get us up so early; you were young once, too."

As a parent, you are being asked to make loads of decisions: Can your teenager go to this film? Can they stay up that late? Sometimes, decisions are being made without consulting you, or in spite of consulting you. All this puts *you* under pressure. Try to make informed decisions. Many of the teenagers we have spoken to say they get a blanket 'no' to many requests. We know that's their perspective, but if they can see you are making informed decisions they will respect you for it – whatever they say to us! If you simply use a blanket 'no', it's likely that they'll find a way to disobey, anyway.

"Give us more freedom. Trust us."

Talk to other parents to help you make decisions about issues like pocket money. That will give you information when you're told that 'everyone else…' It will also mean that you're treating them fairly.

How much responsibility do you want to give them, for example, independence about bus fares and lunches? What about clothing? And going out? Again, communication is the key.

"Please try to be a bit more open-minded about things. Don't be so protective and boss me around so much."

How can you help your children to find an appropriate time and space to do homework? It might not be the way you would do it! Again, the key is to help them find something that works for them.

…and now for the really helpful bit It's a two-way relationship. One of the Ten Commandments is 'Respect your father and your mother'. Yet even in the early church, there was clearly some parent–child conflict because as well as **telling the children to obey their parents, Paul also had to tell the Ephesian dads not to exasperate their children (Ephesians 6:1–4). Some things never change, then!**

NOTE TO PARENTS

"TRY NOT TO GET SO FRUSTRATED."

One of the greatest things you can offer your children is to encourage their freedom to develop relationships with other trusted adults. There will be many things that they would prefer to talk about openly with someone who is not their mum or dad.

Priorities

You want your child to have *the* best start in life. Education is a real key to that. However, education isn't everything, and it's equally important that they have a life outside school. The balance of that is hard to juggle, but it's probably no harder than your desire to juggle the balance between home and work. Working together to create some kind of balance is a huge investment in your child's future. Too much emphasis on education runs the risk of creating a workaholic adult… or someone ready to pack it all in.

Be there

You have invested heavily in your children up to now. They will try things that worry you, scare you, and make you angry. Trust in the investment that you have made in them, and slowly begin to let them go.

This book contains loads of ideas and insights from a Christian perspective into handling the many facets which make up teenage life. In the end, the most significant thing you can do is to be there – whatever happens.

Key to Symbols Used in This Book

TIPS get practical help on the issues that matter to you. Heaps of ideas you can try right now.

GOD hear from God with relevant Bible bits and verses.

FLASH flashes of inspiration or info that might help get things into perspective.

CASE HISTORY read about other people's experiences. You may be going through something similar!

Intro: Stress!

"I'm stressed! Stop putting pressure on me!"

How many times have you thought that this week? Or heard someone else say it? What does it mean to be stressed? What does it feel like? Where does stress come from? What makes *you* feel under pressure? What can you do about it? And where does God fit in?

"I am stressed by periods, parents, friends and especially my brother and sister!"

What worries you?

If something stresses you, then it does. It doesn't matter if it doesn't bother anyone else. This is about you. So, what bothers *you*?

- [ ] Spiders
- [ ] Feeling incompetent in class
- [ ] Emergencies
- [ ] Talking to people I don't know
- [ ] Being on my own
- [ ] Having to talk in front of lots of people
- [ ] Meeting deadlines with school work
- [ ] People arguing and shouting
- [ ] When a pet dies
- [ ] Something else (...)

People react in very different ways. How do *you* react?
- [ ] I throw my mobile phone.
- [ ] I go off by myself.
- [ ] I either just stop talking or start yelling for no reason.
- [ ] I end up snapping at my family.
- [ ] I stomp around... but it doesn't work!
- [ ] I feel sick and sometimes have panic attacks.
- [ ] I'm rude to other people because whatever they do annoys me.
- [ ] I...

Physical phacts

"Stress is very stressful!"

A little bit of stress can be good for you. If you never had any pressure at all, you'd be a blob of jelly. Stress keeps your body alert and it motivates you. Did you ever have one of those stocking-filler gadgets, which were propelled by a rubber band? The right amount of tension makes the machine go like a dream. Too much tension makes the rubber band snap. Too much stress can make us snap. And there's plenty around. Too much stress can make you:
- [ ] feel tired.
- [ ] ache all over.
- [ ] cry and feel sad.
- [ ] have panic attacks.
- [ ] have broken sleep.
- [ ] suffer from stomach upsets.
- [ ] feel sick.
- [ ] have itchy skin rashes.
- [ ] more likely to get colds and flu.
- [ ] fiddle.

"It creates a bad atmosphere in the house."

It's easy to think that you're in control of stress and pressure. But if it all gets too much, you can lose control as you try to release the tension. Sometimes that means that people turn to drugs or alcohol, stealing or other things that are completely out of character. Learn to deal with stress before it gets out of control. If you don't, you'll have to live with the consequences.

What can I do about it?
Loads! First of all, tell someone. Tell God; tell your mum; tell a mate; tell the cat. Bottling everything up inside isn't going to help.

Then think about what makes you feel good. It might be sport, fishing, listening to music, praying, chilling out with friends, stroking your pet, talking to Gran. Whatever is a good stress reliever for you, make time to fit it into your week.

Your body is the packaging you live in, and it needs to be looked after. You can improve how you feel by eating healthy food (fruit and veg!), drinking plenty of water or squash, getting some exercise and getting enough sleep. The foods that you might crave when you're feeling low – like sugary snacks and fizzy drinks – will only make you feel better for a short time. And then they might make you feel worse. That's science for you!

 ...and now for the really helpful bit Sometimes reading about Jesus makes him seem superhuman. But he experienced all our human feelings. Just before he was arrested (Luke 22:44), he went to the Mount of Olives, as usual, and prayed. 'Jesus was in great pain and prayed so sincerely that his sweat fell to the ground like drops of blood.' Jesus was under extreme stress. He knew he had to face a vicious death – as God, Jesus was all-knowing, and he must also have read the Old Testament prophecies which talked about it. He struggled to see if there was another way. And, in the end, he trusted God and found a way through a most terrible death.

You'll always have some stress. Even when you look after your body well, there's plenty of room for unpredictable hormones and stuff that will happen to you. But the more you take care of yourself, the more you can reduce the impact which stress can have.

Big changes

Some things which put pressure on us are predictable – exams, people at school, parents, even huge changes, like moving school or moving house. Other pressures can come from nowhere fast – divorce, death, war and so on. If you're a Christian, then you have some stuff in the Bible that will help you to deal with life's changes, even if they are unpredictable. You may have parents, friends and other adults to whom you can talk. Also, you have access to God – who, unlike your parents, isn't stressed!

If you're going through big changes, remember that it's quite normal to feel rather lost on the way. The key is always to find a trustworthy adult to talk to.

Under Pressure is a chance to look at different things which stress people and see how we might handle them. Believe it or not, there are plenty of ideas in the Bible about coping with stress. If you think that your parents don't understand what you're going through, get them to read this book. And then you might want to talk about it together.

Tough Stuff: Dealing With Loss

Help! I can't cope!

As much as we might want everything always to be the same, it isn't. Things change, some for the better and some for the worse. Whether it's moving house, someone dying or people separating, life can be difficult to cope with for a while. Many of the feelings we have at times of loss are the same for all these big events, and there are different ways to cope. The most important thing is to find someone to talk to whom you trust and who will listen.

Everyone has losses. Sometimes a loss is close to you; sometimes it's further away. It can be tough to handle, especially when other people at school are carrying on normally and may have no idea what you're thinking or feeling. We all think bad things can't happen to us. Sometimes they do.

"When my mum was diagnosed with cancer, I realised that we're all just mortal."

The grieving process

Everyone reacts individually, but there tends to be a typical pattern in the grieving process. Shock usually comes first. You may try to pretend nothing has happened. Then you get angry. You think life isn't fair. You may even get angry at the person who is sick or who has died. Sometimes you feel a lot of regrets. You say: 'If only I'd done this or not done that.' Later, you feel sad. It can be really confusing to go through these feelings, and they may last a long time. But you need to go through them so that you can move on.

"I started to feel snappy. No one else knew I was feeling like this."

When you're dealing with loss, it's important to talk with someone you trust about what happened, about your feelings and your memories. Not every friend can understand. You might need an adult to help – a parent, a teacher you trust, or your minister or youth leader. **You will get through tough times and be even stronger for it – if you talk.**

Moving away

"I wanted to go to this new school, but I still find it hard to have left the old one."

Whether you're moving house, school, church or something else, there's always a time lag between the change happening and your feelings catching up with you.

"I cried a lot before I went to secondary school."

However much you want to do it, most people find it scary to leave what they know and go out into a new place.

"My mum got stressed out. I try and avoid her when she's in a bad mood."

Some people cry; others look fine – but you can be sure they have a few wobbly times!

"I was OK. My parents weren't."

"I worried about getting my head flushed down the toilet." "And was it?" "No!"

...and now for the really helpful bit One of the biggest changes in the Bible was for the Israelites to leave Egypt and move to the Promised Land. Egypt was awful, and they were treated badly. The wilderness was safer, and God provided what they needed. They still found it tough, and complained like crazy. It was 40 years before they moved into the new place.

It won't take you 40 years to adapt to a move, but it will take some time! After the shock of a big change hits you, you'll be encouraged to look to the future – whether it's a great new school or a new family situation. But you also need time to sort out what's happening and catch up with yourself.

Think about what you're losing. If you're upset, that's OK. Find someone you can cry on, shout at or be silent with.

"I got lost once, but a year 8 showed me where to go."

If it's bothering you, then it's bothering you, and you need to be able to say that. It doesn't mean the move is wrong. You're just catching up.

What's over? And what isn't? Who are the friends you want to keep in touch with? Can you fix up a sleepover or a get-together now so that you have something to look forward to? Will you phone, text, write (!?!) or chat on MSN?

What are you taking with you from the old place? It might be a photo, an old school shirt, or anything which reminds you of the good times.

> It can be helpful to mark an ending in some way. If you're leaving a school, or moving house, you might put on a bit of a party.

Once you've done that, even when you are in your new life and doing normal stuff, you may well still feel a bit confused, fed up or weepy. This is NORMAL.

"We've moved churches and my mum doesn't know anyone."

It takes time for people to move on from one thing to the next. It may take days or weeks. But it's OK.

UNDER PRESSURE

Hang in there, work on the stuff that's coming up for you and you'll find that the new beginning does come. However hard you find it, the secret is to keep talking to someone.

Piggy in the Middle

"My mum and dad are getting a divorce. I feel trapped in the middle."

When any relationship stops working, it can be very sad. No longer being friends with someone, or breaking up with a girlfriend/boyfriend can be a very tough time. However, probably the worst break-up that can happen is if your parents divorce.

"When my parents argue, I think about what would happen if they divorced. Who would I go with? I am worried because they argue a lot."

TOUGH STUFF

Every relationship has its ups and downs, and every relationship has its arguments. In fact, experts tell us that arguments can be healthy because you tend to say what you feel, and being honest with people is good.

Arguments often sound a lot worse to those listening.

However, sometimes two people are just not able to get on with each other any more. And if living with someone is making life miserable and sad, then maybe it is better that they don't live with each other any more.

You are not responsible for your parents' relationship. However, your parents are responsible for their relationship with you, and you are responsible for your relationship with them.

If something is worrying you about what your parents are doing, then tell them. Maybe they are unaware that their behaviour is affecting you in such a way. Tell them that their arguing worries you. You are part of the family, and your feelings are important!

It can be destructive to live in the past, wishing your parents were still together. You may find it helpful to talk about your feelings with your parents or another trustworthy adult, so that you can move on and try to find some good things about your current situation.

"WHEN THEY FIRST GOT DIVORCED, I DIDN'T WANT IT TO HAPPEN. BUT IT'S BETTER NOW. IT'S A LOT BETTER. THEY ARE BOTH HAPPIER WITH THEIR NEW PARTNERS. IT WAS A GOOD THING TO HAPPEN."

17

Although a divorce may be right for your parents, it doesn't mean that it will be easy for you. Seeing two people whom you love being upset with each other is very hard. And parents need to understand that a divorce is a huge thing for their children to accept.

> "It's hard because one lets us do something and the other doesn't. So now I just say: 'This is a mum day – I can do this,' or: 'This is a dad day – I can do that.'"

Divorce means change. It may mean a change of house, a change of routine and a change of relationship with one parent. Be open with both parents about how you feel about these changes. If something is not working, say so. For example, if you're not happy hopping to different houses every weekend, say so.

...and now for the really helpful bit The Bible asks big things of us, especially when it comes to other people. It says that we should be 'humble and gentle. Patiently put up with each other and love each other' (Ephesians 4:2). Colossians 3:13 says: 'Put up with each other, and forgive anyone who does you wrong, just as Christ has forgiven you.' Finally, 1 Corinthians 13:5 says that true love does not keep a record of wrongs that others do. Forgiveness – being able to continue to love both parents and to accept their decision – is difficult and it is painful.

Jesus said that we shouldn't judge other people (Matthew 7:1–5). It's easy to make judgements based on what we see (or hear!), but we don't know what else is going on. When the Bible says that we should honour our parents, that doesn't only apply if they are together. It's also true if they are separated or divorced. And if you're asked to take sides, you can always say: 'That's not my call!'

Divorce often means that one or both parents will meet new people, and possibly get married. So in a short time you could go from two parents at home, down to one, and then have a whole new family: new parent, new brothers and sisters and new grandparents. It can be stressful trying to adjust to the changes involved, and you may feel angry with one or both of your parents for their behaviour.

"I can get jealous when my step-sister says 'my dad'. But I get two lots of holidays and two lots of birthday presents."

Never bottle up your feelings, and whether you go to your parent, a mature friend, or a church leader, always try to find someone to talk through how you are feeling.

 …and now for the really helpful bit

Whatever else happens in your family, you need to know who you are. Although you have imperfect parents, you need to know that in heaven you have a perfect parent – a Father who will never let you down, never leave you, never forget you and will always love you perfectly. That's a promise that Jesus has given YOU. He says that he will '*be with you always, even until the end of the world*' (Matthew 28:20).

In the Bible, Paul says that when you become a Christian, your family changes. Yes, you still have an earthly family, but that may break up, disappear or even die! As a Christian, you are adopted into God's family. You are God's child. God now regards you and treats you as a son or a daughter. And that means you will receive *all* the promises of God (Galatians 3:26–29). So, you are secure in a family which will always have you, always love you and always be with you, regardless of what happens. Even if you get new step-sisters, step-brothers, or a step-mum or step-dad, and you feel left out, remember your heavenly family. And you might find lots of security from a friend's family, or from trustworthy people in your church.

Sometimes Christian parents divorce. You might move out of the church and lose your church base. Have a look at the chapter about moving, for some ideas about what you can do to get some good support from Christian people during this time. Talk to your youth leader or another Christian adult whom you trust.

TOUGH STUFF

I wish I were immortal

"I'm so scared of dying because I'm not really sure if heaven exists."

"I used to dream about dying. Everything went black. I couldn't talk to anyone. I couldn't move."

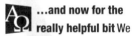 **…and now for the really helpful bit** We don't know 100 per cent what happens when people die, but there are plenty of signposts in the Bible. Jesus was a man, and we know that he died and rose from death in the same body he lived in. Then he went to heaven. He's the model, from the Christian point of view, of what happens when we die. We don't know exactly what to expect, but we can trust Jesus (John 14:1–4): 'Don't be worried! Have faith in God and have faith in me. There are many rooms in my Father's house. I wouldn't tell you this, unless it was true. I am going there to prepare a place for each of you. After I have done this, I will come back and take you with me. Then we will be together.' That sounds good to me!

"It's one of those things I think about when I'm lying in bed with nothing to do. I'm more scared about what might happen to make me die."

"I worry about dying before my parents. Would they cope?"

Funerals, wakes and other barrels of laughs

"MY FRIEND'S GRANDAD DIED AND IT'S MADE ME THINK ABOUT DEATH A LOT. I DON'T LIKE IT."

Medical science has become so hi-tech and so developed that it's easy to start thinking that death is a failure. It feels as though doctors should be able to sort out everything. But they can't. The only thing that *everyone* will do is die. Only one person in history died, came back to life and stayed alive for ever – and that was Jesus Christ.

"IT'S TABOO. IF I WENT TO TALK TO SOMEONE ABOUT DEATH, THEY'D THINK I WAS WEIRD."

The death of a family member or friend can come as a big shock, especially when it happens unexpectedly. As well as being upset that someone has suffered, we also start to ask some hard questions: Why did it happen? What will we miss about this person? What will never be the same? What will happen when *we* die?

As well as expecting people always to get better, we've also been led to expect answers. Sometimes there just aren't any answers. Why is someone suffering? Why them and not someone else?

...and now for the really helpful bit Even Jesus went through moments when he asked that unanswerable question. On the cross, he cried out: 'My God, my God, why have you deserted me?' (Mark 15:34)

"I FELT REALLY BAD THAT I HADN'T GOT TO KNOW HER BETTER. AND BECAUSE I WAS more upset when my dog died."

"if my parents die, will i be taken into care?"

 ...and now for the really helpful bit

Christians believe that there is life after death. We don't know what that is like – it may not all be fluffy clouds and angels – but we know that it says in the Bible that 'Adam brought death to all of us, and Christ will bring life to all of us' (1 Corinthians 15:22). And without Christ, death is the process which separates us from God. Jesus said that God loved the people of this world so much that he sent his Son to live on earth, so that everyone who believes in Jesus will never really die, but have everlasting life. So death doesn't have to separate us from God any more. And if you want to know what everlasting life looks like, you'll have to wait and see!

I don't understand why it happens. That person wasn't bad.

When God created his world, he could have filled it with robots that went around obeying their computer chips without having any capacity to think. But he didn't. We were created with the ability to make choices and decisions. Choice has consequences. So, for example, when the Twin Towers collapsed in New York, the people who died weren't to blame. They died because of choices that the hijackers made. And the hijackers made those choices because of what other people had said or done in the past.

"my mum died. it annoys me when people argue with their mums. i say, 'don't do it!'"

Suffering

Sometimes people get hurt, or become ill, or are born with huge problems for no apparent reason. Some things just happen. It sounds a really glib thing to say, but unfortunately it's true – some things do just happen. But, to an extent, we can choose how we are going to react to them.

In 1993, a bomb in the north of England killed a teenager and a young boy. Their parents chose to make the best out of what had happened, and a huge peace centre has been started to help children and young people work together for peace and against conflict. Those parents could have

chosen to stay angry at God and at the world. They will still be sad to have lost their children. But imagine how excited they must feel now when they look at the hundreds of young people whose lives have been changed by the work that they have set up. Although those families suffered so much when their children died, they chose to make something from it.

Sometimes we can just continue to hurt ourselves by staying still and staying angry, and being unable to move through problems and difficulties.

If bad stuff is happening to us or to people we know, we can pray for strength to get through it and we can talk to people we trust. We can also pray for God to make something positive come from suffering. Prayer makes a difference. It connects our pain and confusion with God. Then, instead of only looking at our own feelings, we have a bigger picture.

God doesn't send earthquakes and bombs to punish bad people. And he doesn't send a Superman-style rescue attempt to save innocent people. When we pray and ask God for help, he gives it. But it can come in unexpected ways.

…and now for the really helpful bit Jesus did nothing wrong. Ever. And he suffered. 'He was silent like a lamb being led to the butcher …' (Isaiah 53:7)

Big Stuff: Pressures from the World We Live in

Bombs and Big News

"I get really scared about stuff I see in the news."

Sometimes we enjoy watching films or reading books that are a bit scary. However, today's 24-hour TV and radio news coverage means that we can hear step-by-step news of the bad things that are happening around the world. Sometimes we worry more than is reasonable. We hear about wars, terrorism and global epidemics like SARS, and the dangers can seem immediate and overwhelming.

In reality, although you are quite likely to have your mobile phone or your bike stolen, you are extremely unlikely to get caught up in a global epidemic, a war or a terrorist act. And you are very unlikely to be attacked or abducted, although these are the crimes which attract high-profile reporting. We don't hear enough good news, which means that it's easy to get scared that the world is a much more dangerous place than it really is.

BIG STUFF

 …and now for the really helpful bit Guess what? Nothing's new. Even 2,000 years ago, Jesus told his disciples: 'You will soon hear about wars and threats of wars, but don't be afraid. These things will have to happen first, but that isn't the end. Nations and kingdoms will go to war against each other. People will starve to death, and in some places there will be earthquakes.' (Matthew 24:6–7)

At any time, there are wars going on all over the world. The TV covers some, sometimes, especially when our own nations are involved. When it gets close to home, such as in the war with Iraq, we might fear for our own safety.

"WHEN THE TWIN TOWERS COLLAPSED, THE EVENT SEEMED TO AFFECT PEOPLE PARTICULARLY DEEPLY."

What can I do?

If you are afraid, talk about it with someone. During the Iraq war, many people in the UK felt afraid that missiles would land here. However, the air attacks were all within a small radius of Iraq, and we were safe from missile attack in the UK.

So, if you are feeling stressed by world events:

- ☑ Check out the facts. Are you worrying about facts? Or are you worrying about impossibilities?
- ☑ Remember that events make the headlines because they are unusual. They don't happen every day.
- ☑ Talk to your friends about what's worrying you.
- ☑ Talk to your teacher or youth leader. Often it's the thoughts in your head which are frightening you the most. Getting it out can release the pressure.
- ☑ If you can't sleep, tell your parents.
- ☑ If you need old ted, find him!
- ☑ And try not to listen to the news late at night.

What about news closer to home?

"ALMOST EVERY SUMMER THERE'S A BIG NEWS STORY ABOUT A CHILD BEING MURDERED BY A STRANGER. AND THERE'S SOMETIMES STUFF IN THE NEWS ABOUT TEENAGERS MEETING UP WITH CHAT ROOM FRIENDS AND BEING TAKEN."

"I'M SCARED IF I SEE SOMEONE WITH A HOOD ON."

There's no need to be terrified. It's very unlikely that anything like that will happen to you but it's important to be sensible. A few precautions can help you to keep safe. And even if you believe in God, you also need to be practical and take care of yourself!

Stay smart

- ☑ Think before you decide to go somewhere – how will you get back home?
- ☑ Stay in a big group.
- ☑ If you have an argument and split from your mates, phone home. This isn't the time to try and be cool!
- ☑ Never think you're tough enough.
- ☑ Keep your mobile with you – but not too obvious.
- ☑ Keep spare change in case you need to use a phone box.
- ☑ Make sure you're near other people.
- ☑ Never get in a car with someone unless you've cleared it with your mum or dad. Ask your parents who you can always go with… then check with them on the day about anyone else.
- ☑ Walk in front of houses, not in alleys.

Remember to be as streetwise on the Internet as you are anywhere else:

- ☑ Never give your name or personal details to people in a chat room.
- ☑ It is unwise to arrange to meet anyone you have spoken to in a chat room. If you do, *always, always* go with an adult.
- ☑ If you access porn or other adult sites by mistake, close them straight away.
- ☑ Don't ever talk dirty with anyone on line.
- ☑ There is more to life than cyber-surfing – do real-life stuff as well!

So try to keep everything in context. And remember that you can have a life and still be safe. It's good to go out and have a bit of responsibility. Just be sensible.

WORRIES ABOUT THE ENVIRONMENT

Should we be green?

Someone once said that the problem we have about the environment is that although we need to get rid of stuff, we have discovered that nothing really goes away.

Try as we might, we cannot get rid of our waste. If we try and burn it, it goes into our atmosphere. If we try and bury it, it pollutes our land. We put it in the ocean and it pollutes our seas.

This can make us feel worried about the future of the planet – and has created a huge interest in green issues. Recycling is now the 'in thing'. You can have loads of different bins outside your door: one for real rubbish, one for newspapers, one for vegetable peelings, one for cans or bottles and so on.

"Litter really annoys me!"

As Christians, what should our attitude be to the environment?

...and now for the really helpful bit God gave planet earth to the human race as a gift – he told Adam to take care of it and look after it (Genesis 2:15).

Eden was to be a place where Adam and his children could grow, learn and develop, and be in a relationship with God. That was the point of planet earth. As we know, things took a different turn.

God intended us to explore, to eat and to use the earth's resources. In Genesis 1:28–30, God gives Adam permission to bring the earth under his control. Adam was to rule over the fish, the birds and the animals. The resources of the earth were meant to be used by the human race. The problem has been that as the human race has grown and developed, we are using the resources more quickly than they can be replaced.

One day, the earth will pass away – it will be no more (Revelation 21:1–2). If the earth that we are now living on is going to end, God must have known this when he created Adam and Eve and put them in the Garden of Eden; he must have known that one day this planet would have served its purpose and would no longer be needed.

We don't have any record of Jesus ever mentioning environmental problems, because they weren't an issue then. We shouldn't be trying to preserve the planet; we should be asking how we are getting on with the original request: *to take care of it, and to look after it.*

If you gave someone a gift and said to them, 'Look after it,' how would you feel if you came back a while later and found that they had wrecked the gift, smashed it and tried to tape it back together?

"Can't someone else do it?"
(*Homer Simpson's campaign slogan to be Environment Minister.*)

So how can I be green?
- ☑ Think before you buy.
- ☑ Use renewable resources where you can.
- ☑ Say no to extra plastic bags if you go shopping.
- ☑ Recycle and reuse whenever you can.
- ☑ And as you make more choices as a consumer, think about the effect they have on the environment, as well as the price!

Maybe the earth will pass away one day. If that's the case, it will be in God's timing. Meanwhile, we can choose to **take care of our planet and look after it by the way we live. That is a gift to God – and a gift to others.**

And what about global warming? Well, what about it? Remember, God is in charge of the world and he knows exactly what's going on. That means *we* don't have to worry about it. We can just trust in God because he knows what he's doing.

UNDER PRESSURE

"Good-enough" stuff: Dealing with the pressure to succeed

It's Monday again

"If I've had a bad day at school, I can't be bothered to talk."

"I pray about school work all the time. But it's still too hard!"

School is important. Learning is good – but it is not the only thing in the world. Tests and exams are not the ultimate test of how intelligent you are. Some people can do them, and some find them almost impossible. It doesn't necessarily show how brainy you are. A lot of pressure is placed on you at school. Perhaps too much. And whatever happens in exams now, there is always the possibility of coming back to education later.

"Teachers are trying their best under difficult circumstances."

💡 Exams assume that *everyone* has reached the same stage at the same time. Not so: people develop in

"GOOD-ENOUGH" STUFF

different ways and at different speeds. You may achieve more outside school than inside school. The important thing is to do your best and achieve your potential. Qualifications are earned not just in school but also at evening classes, sixth-form colleges, correspondence courses, on-line courses and adult education classes.

 ...and now for the really helpful bit There are some things you just don't want to do. And some things which you are better at than others. Paul told some people: 'Do your work willingly, as though you were serving the Lord himself …' (Colossians 3:23). You know that if you do that, even with something you find really hard, you'll be doing your very best. So next time you have *that* homework, sit down and do it as though you were doing it for God.

"Mum says that as long as I do my best, it doesn't matter because she will still love me."

School *is* important – but it's not the end of the world if you don't achieve all the goals set for you – or even if you fail. As a youth worker, I've been shocked at how little social life young people have because of the need to finish assignments and homework. Learning Maths, English and Science is important, but it is not everything! Imagine! Some people study and take exams from the age of 11 until they are 21. Then, once they have finished university, they may be in the workplace until they are 65 years old. Pressure from 11 to 65. Eek! Learning to relax about it now is an important start!

 Andy says: 'I hated school – I tried everything not to go. My teachers told my mum that I would never amount to much in

33

life. I was a D student. I left school at 16 with three exam passes. I failed at school. Yet it was not until I had left school that I began to enjoy learning. At 25, I went to university, having never taken an A-level in my life, and came away three years later with a degree.'

HOMEWORK

"I get so much homework, I never get any time to myself."

It's true: you do have loads of homework. You are the most tested generation. That's what the newspapers and experts say. No other generation of young people has had to go through as many exams and tests as you. You get significantly more homework than your parents did. With coursework on top of that, it all adds up. And, whether you like it or not, it will need to be done. So how do you manage it all?

Coping strategies

"More and more work is piled onto us."

Well, you can choose how to do it! What is better for you: to leave it all

"GOOD-ENOUGH" STUFF

until the last minute but worry about it all the time? Or to do it now? Then you can relax and enjoy yourself afterwards. How can you best manage your time so that you get it all done and still have time to do other stuff? This is all basic stuff, but it *can* make a difference.

💡 The three steps

1. The first step is to find the best starting time, so that you have cleared your head after school but so that homework doesn't drag on and on into the evening.
2. The second is to get rid of all distractions.
3. And the third is to find a good place to work.

When you come in from school, what do you need to do to chill? You could have a drink and a snack, and maybe change out of your uniform. Do whatever it takes to sort yourself out before it's homework time!

And then come the distractions! What are they? Your mobile, the phone, MSN, the TV, family, friends, computer games, magazines, radio… the list of distractions is endless. They could all mean that it's 8pm and your mum's still saying (or nagging!): 'Have you done your homework?'

> "Mum tells me to do this. Dad tells me to do that. And I get told off."

You know the distractions which are going to stop *you* working. So do something about them. Remember that the friends who distract you during the day will probably be the same ones who distract you after you get home!

💡 You can always video *Neighbours*! If you plan your work around your TV viewing, that will stop you

35

having 30 minutes to work now… and then 45 minutes after the next programme…

If you can't bear to cut yourself off from people, say you can only talk for five minutes (*max!*) then ask if they can call back later.

As Nike say: 'Just do it!' That way, your homework will get done! If you can manage time effectively, you really will get more free time. Computer games can wait. If you don't mark out time for homework, it will end up splodging over all your free time – like a melted ice cream.

So where's a good place to work?

If you work in your bedroom, try and organise some clear space where you can spread out your stuff and think clearly. If you tidy work up and put it back in your bag when you've finished, you won't have to look at it all the time.

If the best place to work is another room in the house, ask the rest of the family for their support.

You may find that you just can't work at home. If you have lots of brothers and sisters, there's no point getting mad at them when they're noisy – it will just stress *you* out even more! See if your school runs a homework or after-school club, or spend some time in the public library.

It is important to accept that you have hundreds of nights of homework ahead (sorry!), and if you can find something that works for you early on, it will really help you. And any good habits you start now will be a great help later, when you may want to put other stuff into your week as well – perhaps parties, driving lessons, or a part-time job.

So there you are with the homework. The whole evening stretches ahead! If the teacher has set 30 minutes, try and do the work in 30 minutes. You could take the whole evening but a skill which is good to develop is doing a task in the time available. Occasionally you'll need to overrun, but it's a good principle to start with. It will also make you start in the first place!

Some days you will have less homework than you expected. Have an evening off and do something different. Or do a bit of tomorrow's homework… Now there's a thought!

"I feel stressed when my parents nag about homework all the time and it's like they think school's the most important thing in the world."

Everyone works in a different way. Some people can just sit down and work for half an hour on one subject and be finished. Other people work better in small chunks. If small chunks work for you, try rotating three subjects and start off by doing ten minutes on each. Then, after the first half-hour, go back to the first subject again and do a bit more. And stop when you still have more to say. Then, when you come back to it, you'll be full of enthusiasm… and you won't be staring at the wall!

"Parents nag because you haven't done your homework. If you do it, then you get a reputation for doing it and they leave you alone to get on with it!"

SATS and exams – groan!

Every time you think you've done them, more exams or SATS tests seem to come round the corner. SATS are tests to see how the school and the teachers are getting on. For you, they are just a measurement – it's like measuring your height or your shoe size.

But it doesn't feel like that, does it? There's loads of pressure from parents and teachers to do well. And school can become a place obsessed by TESTS! In fact, most teachers are unhappy about the pressure all this places on you, but they have to do what is set by the government, which has decided this is what you need.

"TEACHERS PUT YOU UNDER PRESSURE TO GET GOOD MARKS BECAUSE OF GOVERNMENT STATS. BAD RESULTS CAN REFLECT ON TEACHERS – EVEN IF THEY'RE REALLY GOOD."

...and now for the really helpful bit Jesus was tested by local government all the time (Matthew 16:1–4). They were always asking him to 'do this'. And then 'do that'. In a way, he did everything they asked him to do, but he interpreted it in his way and didn't let his life be ruled by all that testing.

There's plenty you can do to help you cope with stress during test or exam time:
- ☑ Take small breaks throughout the day to do something else.
- ☑ Get plenty of sleep.
- ☑ Try not to do too much work each day.
- ☑ Have a life outside school!
- ☑ Eat plenty of fresh fruit and vegetables (boring but true!).
- ☑ Get some exercise – walking, playing sport, dancing etc.

"I can't sleep. I lie awake at night thinking about exams."

On exam or test days, a few simple things can really help:

- ☑ Go to the toilet before the test or exam starts.
- ☑ Sit quietly and pray or focus before you begin the exam.
- ☑ Remember: this isn't about coming top – it's about doing your best and achieving your potential.
- ☑ When you see a question you can't answer, don't panic! Take a few deep breaths and have another look. If you're still stuck, move on to another question and come back later.
- ☑ It's always better to write something than to leave a blank.
- ☑ And in the end, just do your best.

Time and space

"I'm fed up. It's all pressure, pressure, pressure."

As we've already said, a little bit of stress can help motivate you. It's too much stress that can be mind-bending.

Stress is nothing new. In 450BC, Herodotus said: 'If a man insisted always on being serious, and never allowed himself a bit of fun and relaxation, he would go mad or become unstable without knowing it.'

So what do you do for fun? Write it down over the page.

UNDER PRESSURE

_____

_____

_____

_____

_____

_____

You may enjoy listening to music, hanging out with friends, reading. Or you may like fishing, playing a musical instrument, art, sculpture, making clothes.

"MY ENGLISH TEACHER SAYS: 'REMEMBER: EVERYONE NEEDS TO BE A MORON FOR FIVE MINUTES A DAY. WATCH TELETUBBIES AND FORGET THERE'S A REAL WORLD!'"

No time? Well, what *is* filling up your time at the moment? If you just can't work out where the time goes, keep a record of how you spend *all* your time over the next few days. Then you can choose to stop doing some things, or do them differently, so that you can make time to do what you want to do… or to do nothing.

Managing the pressures

You don't have to find something to do every moment of every day, but doing nothing all the time can be quite stressful, too! So where's the in-between? Here are some ideas that you might find helpful to manage some of your daily pressures.

Just say no

Do you ever feel guilty about saying no to people? The trouble is: if we keep on saying yes, we can end up under a huge heap of stuff to do. And how does that feel? Well, it's heavy, isn't it? And it's not much fun!

"GOOD-ENOUGH" STUFF

 Brother Lawrence was a seventeenth-century monk. His companions had a rule of life – a sort of 'ten helpful hints to live a godly life'. 'For us, planned neglect will mean deliberately choosing what things we will leave undone or postpone, so that instead of being oppressed by a clutter of unfinished jobs, we think out our priorities under God, and accept, without guilt or resentment, the fact that much we had thought we ought to do, we must leave.'

Sometimes, choosing to leave things undone is the only way. So, if you choose to leave your English homework until next week, the key is to stop thinking about it until it's time to start doing it! Keeping a diary is a good way of remembering what you've decided to do when.

Slow down

Are you always running around doing everything really quickly? It's even got a name now: Speed Living! How about trying to do everything more slowly sometimes? And don't forget to breathe!

Jesus often took time out with his friends to get away from the pressures of life in first-century Palestine.

Enjoy today

You are driven by deadlines – next week, next term, after options, after SATS… It's easy to be so busy thinking about tomorrow that you never have time to enjoy today. Remember that time in Year 6 between SATS and the end of term? You could choose to think only about leaving school… or you could choose to enjoy all the fun stuff that the teachers let you do.

...and now for the really helpful bit Jesus said: 'Don't worry about tomorrow. It will take care of itself.' (Matthew 6:34)

The sound of silence
Does 'peace and quiet' sound like something only your gran would enjoy? Think again…

Try turning off the music, the TV, the DVD and your mobile… and be silent for just a minute. Christians are much better at singing about silence than actually doing it! But you'll be amazed how it can clear your head.

> "Be still, and know that I am God…"
> *Psalm 46:10 (NIV)*

...and now for the really helpful bit Silence is a great way to start praying or reading the Bible. Prayer is about communicating with God – talking to him *and* listening.

Safety net
Have you ever been to the circus? The high-wire acts are awesome. And they always have a safety net! Sometimes when we feel under pressure, it can feel like walking on the high wire (I think! I haven't actually done it). The circus artists know that if they fall, there is something to protect them. Do you know that? What's your safety net when the pressure is on? Belief in God is an important one, and so is a sympathetic and helpful teacher, a parent, a youth leader or a good mate.

Know where your safety net is before you need it!

There's more to life than…

If it all gets too much, remember:
There's more to life than
homework/trainers/options etc.

> What's stressing you out at the moment? Write it below:

There's more to life than...

_____

_____

_____

_____

_____

PRESSURE FROM PARENTS

"We only want what's best for you…"

"My parents are obsessed with my education. I think I'm doing fine but they stop me going out with friends or watching TV, even when I've done my homework."

It is a strange experience becoming a parent. As we write this, I am only a few weeks away from becoming a dad. I am already thinking about what the baby will be like – what will happen when he grows up – what will he do? I am starting to dream dreams about his future. It's hard not to.

These are almost certainly some of the feelings your parents have had for years! They have desires for you – to see you do well, to give you a good start to life in the big wide world. And don't forget that your parents have lived a little longer than you, so they have experienced stuff you haven't. They want you to avoid some of the things they have experienced. They don't want you making the mistakes they made.

> "SOME PARENTS DON'T HELP AT ALL. SOME HELP TOO MUCH."

All of this comes out of the fact that they *love you!* But even a motive of love can cause problems. Often your parents put pressure on you without realising it because their love for you makes them less aware of what's really going on. They want the best for you… but it's not always the same as the best that you want for yourself!

The journey of life

Life is about discovery. Discovering who you are in your family, who you are in the community in which you live, and who you are in God.

Life is also a journey. You don't experience life all at once. If we were to ask you what has been the best moment of your life so far – your answer will be different from the one you would give in five years' time, and different again in a further five years' time. You will experience some wonderful things and you will experience some tragic things. And all of this is part of the journey of living life.

And only *you* can make this journey. People may try to make it for you – but no one can live another person's life. And with any journey that you might go on, you will want to know where to go, what tools are there for helping you on your journey. You need to be able to read signs, and you need to know where to go or what to do if you get lost or stuck.

"They don't push me. If I don't do it, it's my own fault."

Some people want to rush out on the journey all on their own, to experience as much as they can. They refuse any help or advice. They want to experience everything now – 18-certificate films, drink, drugs, sex, money… This can cause problems.

💡 **Your parents should be safety nets – they are the ones who will love and accept you no matter what. They want you to be safe and happy. They are a source of help and information about life. But they cannot live your life. That's your job! If you don't find that love and support at home, you will need to find a trusted and supportive adult who can help you. It might be a relative or someone in your church. It might even be a friend's parent.**

Help! So what can I do?

If your parents are putting pressure on you, you could walk away and do your own thing. But what help would that be – to you or to them? You need to talk to them about how you feel.

💡 **Can you sit down with your parents and talk directly? Or do you have a family friend, the parent of one of your mates, a youth worker or teacher who will listen to you and then come and sit with you as you talk to your parents?**

In an ideal situation, how would you want to spend your time (including enough time to do homework and other stuff)? What needs to happen to get to that point? Are you willing to ask your parents for a trial period until the next exams, to see how it goes?

"If I don't do what she says, my mum might ground me."

Maybe you can agree that you can spend a limited amount of time each day playing computer games, or doing whatever it is you want to do. You'll probably have to give in a little, and so will they!

 ...and now for the really helpful bit In the Bible we are told: 'Children must always obey their parents.' (Colossians 3:20) And then it says: 'Parents, don't be hard on your children. If you are, they might give up.' If you feel that your parents are irritating you beyond what's reasonable, you will need to find some support from another adult if necessary, then begin to negotiate with Mum and Dad.

And bedtime?

"I think 9pm is too early."

Try to have a conversation with your parents about how they have set your bedtime. It might be earlier than you'd like because you are pathologically unable to get up unless you have had ten hours' sleep! In that case – tough!

"Is bedtime when you're sent up? Or when you go to sleep?"

If you really, truly, honestly believe that you can stay up beyond the bedtime your parents have set, then you'll need to negotiate. And be willing to prove it'll work. Why not try asking for a later bedtime once or twice a week? And if you're going to stay up later… remember to be nice to the other people in the house the following day!!

"I want to go to bed when I'm tired."

Sibling Rivalry

Q: What are they?
A: Brothers and sisters.

"My brother got all A* for his exams. Help!"

It's tough to be the oldest. You have to fight all the battles with your parents first. But if you're brainy, your younger brothers and sisters are under huge pressure to be as good as you. The pressure comes from your parents. And from the school. And you can put the pressure on yourself, too.

In fact, the pressure to be like your brothers or sisters – or not like them at all – may be one of the most irritating pressures you face. After all, you'll have been living with each other for a long time. Some of what you feel will be real.

Other people will say things like: 'Don't they look the same?' or: 'You must take after your sister/brother.' Yuck! Even if they're being nice about you, you are still your own person. Living in someone else's shadow can be a nightmare.

'Nobody can make you feel inferior without your consent.' (E. Roosevelt) Is some of the pressure to be like your brother/sister coming from yourself?

...and now for the really helpful bit Esau and Jacob were twins (Genesis 25, 27). They were really different, but the pressure was on because Mum preferred Jacob and Dad preferred Esau. With a few dirty tricks, Mum made sure that her favourite son got Dad's blessing. He became Mr A*.

You may need to train people – your parents and teachers – to understand that you are your own person. Try and be nice about it, and try not to do your brother or sister down.

"IF MY ELDER SISTER HAS DONE WELL, THE TEACHERS NOTICE THE DIFFERENCE BETWEEN US. 'SHE'S NOTHING LIKE HER SISTER,' THEY SAY, 'SHE DOESN'T WORK AS HARD AS HER SISTER.' IF SHE WASN'T MY SISTER, THEY'D LET ME BE ME. AND ACTUALLY, I'M DOING OK."

Your brothers and sisters are unique. There's no one else quite like them. And, most importantly, there's no one else quite like you! Take a look at Psalm 139 if you want to find out how special you are.

Be your own person

The most important thing is that you *do your best and achieve your potential*. Try to negotiate with your parents, and explain what's bothering you.

It might be worth trying some interests and activities which your brother or sister haven't tackled. Bungee jumping it is, then?

Not only is there pressure to be like brothers or sisters, there's also pressure to be like other people at school. You're meant to dress/walk/listen to music like everyone else. It takes huge guts to stick out from the crowd and be you. But in the end, the only way you'll be happy is to be yourself – even if you have to moderate it a bit so you don't stick out too much!!

"IF WE WERE ALL THE SAME, EVERYONE WOULD HAVE BOWL CUTS!"

PRESSURE TO EARN MONEY AND GET A JOB

I don't get enough pocket money. What should I do?

Why do you want to have money? You might get pocket money from your parents, or you might have a paper round, a Saturday job or a babysitting job. But why do you want it?

> "POCKET MONEY IS USUALLY YOUR FIRST STATUS SYMBOL."

Silly question, maybe – you want to buy clothes, top up your mobile, go out and get a Burger King. And you don't want to have to hassle Mum or Dad for money. But money brings a problem: how do you decide how to spend it?

> "PARENTS WANT YOU TO LEARN THE VALUE OF MONEY. I HAVE BASIC POCKET MONEY AND THEN I CAN EARN MORE BY DOING JOBS."

That's not a problem! I just spend it – that's the decision.

When you start to have a bit of money, it's hard going when it runs out and you have to wait until the next pay day. A vicious cycle begins. You do your Saturday job; you get paid; you spend it all by Tuesday, and you have to wait until Saturday. This makes you frustrated. So you borrow money from your parents. Saturday comes, but when you get paid, you have to give back what you've borrowed (if you're a nice person!). And that leaves you with less, so by Sunday, you've spent it all. So you get frustrated and you borrow from your parents and… OK, you get the point. You're stuck in a borrowing cycle.

> "SOCIETY IS DRIVEN BY MONEY AND SO WE NEED TO COME TO TERMS WITH IT."

UNDER PRESSURE

The sad thing is that for some people this cycle lasts most of their working life. And money is an important part of our society. You can't live without it. Money is *not* a bad thing. Money is not a root of all evil. It's the *love* of money which causes all kinds of trouble (1 Timothy 6:10). When you have money you have to decide what to spend it on, how long that money will last you and so on.

"I want more money but I don't want to do a boring job."

 ...and now for the really helpful bit You need to make a decision as soon as you can. Jesus said that nobody (that means *nobody*) can serve two masters. You can either serve God or you can serve money (Matthew 6:24). Serving money is not about having loads of money in your **house and rolling around in piles of bank notes. It's a tad subtler than that. It's about whether you make big life decisions simply around money, for example: 'How much will I get for this?' or: 'I'll do this degree or course because I will earn lots of money.'**

If your reason for living is money, then it's your master. The quicker you make the decision as to who your master will be, the happier (or sadder) you will be.

Now is a great time to get into good habits about money. When you haven't got much, and you can still learn how to save some and give some away, then you're setting good habits for the future.

Imagine getting your salary in air! If every month you were given canisters of air and you had to buy all your food, pay all your bills, as well as have enough air to breathe

50

for a whole week, would you just go out and use all your air in one day? Probably not. You would suffocate very quickly. You would always make sure you had enough air to breathe before you spent any of it!

> "You've got to think in terms of money. Money is power."

It's really, really hard to escape from the pressure to *buy, buy, buy*! About 20 years ago, teenagers asked for hi-fi systems. Now the pressure is on to have a mini system, a TV, a DVD, a PlayStation or a Game Boy, a mobile and even a laptop. And even when you have them, the pressure is back on to have better ones. It's very hard to stand against it and to think what's right for you. And, more importantly, what you or your family can afford. Many Christians don't do this, and end up living a double life. Credit is easy to come by. But debt can easily turn our focus from God to money.

Hang on, did you say give some away?

Yes! Right back in the Old Testament, one of the laws which God gave to Moses was for us to give away a minimum of 10 per cent of everything (Leviticus 27:30). And it's just as important today.

Falling out over money

> "Pocket money's good but it causes rivalry. In my family, it's about how old you are so they always get more than me."

Money can cause people to fall out. Even the simple act of an older brother or sister getting more pocket money can cause the younger one to be jealous. Many adults have killed other people because of money.

Questions to think about if you're desperate for money:
- ✓ Why do you really need the money?
- ✓ Can you cut down what you need?
- ✓ Can you try saving regularly?
- ✓ Can you set up a regular income with odd jobs in future?

So is it OK to have a job? And can I work on a Sunday?

Well, the law has a take on this, depending on where you live. In the UK, you can start a part-time job at 13 and increase working hours once you reach 15. But how do you decide whether to look for a part-time job? (See panel on pros and cons.)

Some people don't get pocket money, and need to have a part-time job to have any cash at all. You will need to decide, together with your parents, what might suit you if you decide to take a job. And some work, like babysitting, is more flexible than a paper round or working in a shop.

"I like going shopping."

But what about Sundays? It's the best day for me, as I've done all my homework by then.

Our 24/7 culture means that nothing much closes, so there are

---

Pros and cons of having a job

Pros
- ✓ Independent money
- ✓ Responsibility
- ✓ Some independence
- ✓ Might get some idea of what you do/don't want to do

Cons
- ✓ Restricts free time, as homework will always take up some time
- ✓ Hard work!
- ✓ May not be very interesting

always jobs which you can do for at least part of every day, including Sunday. If you're ever in doubt about what a gadget can do, look at the instructions. God's instructions (Exodus 20:8–11) say we need to rest on the seventh day. And there are some very good and practical reasons for this. Your body and your brain need a break! Some people have to work Sundays, but God's instructions still clearly state that it's best to have a full day off a week. If you can do that with homework, too, you may well find that you start feeling less pressured.

What next?

How will I ever know what I can do with the rest of my life?

Ask the big questions, why don't you?! Well, very few, if any, people do know what they'll be doing in five, ten or 50 years' time. Fact. I guess that Prince William knows he'll become King of England. Probably. Perhaps. Maybe. But for the rest of us, who knows? In fact, people leaving school now are likely to have five different careers. Not jobs. Careers. Scary! It's stressful to have it all mapped out like Prince William has. Few choices, you see! And it's stressful to have no idea about the future. What you choose at age 14 may be the job you will always do – but it may not. Life changes, often very quickly. You need to make choices with care at 14, but they are not choices which can never be reversed, or changed.

So where does God fit in?

'I will bless you with a future filled with hope – a future of success, not of suffering' (Jeremiah 29:11). We don't need to know the long-term plan now. Imagine having a book in front of you where you could read everything you'd ever do from now until you die. It would drive you nuts. Some Christians say that heaven is our future. To some extent that's right, if we are followers of Jesus. But you're likely to have many years between now and then, and while we're on earth, we're preparing for that time.

...and now for the really helpful bit Take a look at this: 'It's in Christ that we find out who we are and what we are living for. Long before we first heard of Christ and got our hopes up, he had his eye on us, had designs on us for glorious living, part of the overall purpose he is working out in everything and everyone.' (Ephesians 1:11–12, *THE MESSAGE*)

So the first clue is to *know what we are living for*. This gives us much more of a sense of meaning than simply living for money or success. And that's the place to measure whether a job might be a good one for us, or not. It's the grand scale view of where we're going. Over time, you might find that other bits of that picture get clearer. But there's your starter.

Why not start a notebook or computer file, where you begin to dream big dreams about what the future might be. Remember Joseph? Take a look at Genesis chapters 37–47 if you need a reminder. He had big dreams about the future. And his dreams came from God. His dreams helped him get through a really tough time in prison. And, in the end, the future panned out in a most amazing way.

Are you going to live simply to work? Or are you going to work so that you can live a full life – in and outside work? That may be a question for the future. But what about right now? Do you live simply to be educated? Or are you being educated so that you can live a full life?

> Trying to guess what you'll be doing in five or ten years' time can be fun, but it *can* be stressful! Don't always focus on years and years ahead. Plans *always* change.

Help! So where do I begin?

A great start is to be endlessly inquisitive! Ask questions, read stuff, ask people who are doing really interesting jobs if you can shadow them for work experience during the holidays – even for half a day. *Find out some facts*.

Know what you're here for. A common theme throughout the Bible is that significant people knew what they were about. Moses worked tirelessly so that Pharaoh would let God's people go. Nehemiah built a wall. Esther's plan was to save the Jews.

> "I don't know what I want to do. I keep changing my mind. But I'll make sure it's something I want to do."

There is a website which lists over 12,500 careers. Reading it would probably set your head spinning, *but you should know there are many more possibilities than you can imagine*.

And *be open to possibilities*. If you're a computer games whizz, you'll be familiar with games like Tomb Raider where you never know what's on the next level until you get there. That's what your life will be like. Things will come up every so often which open up a completely new world of opportunity.

And you're not in this alone. *Enlist the support of trustworthy adults* who will help you think big. And beware of people who squash your ideas because they wouldn't dare dream. If you really want to be a research scientist, go for it. Equally, if you want to be a plumber, go for it. It may not have such a posh name as research scientist, but if that's what you want, have fun. And everyone needs a plumber!

That's the future. But next year I have to choose my options, and I don't know what to do. It's scary.

The first thing to remember is that there'll be several compulsory subjects, ones that you *have* to do, so you won't have to choose many options yourself.

This may be the first time that you've ever had to make a choice and leave something behind. Even if you've already given up some other activities, like ballet or karate, when you choose options you *have* to leave something behind.

"I feel pressured in case I choose the wrong subject."

Remember: you are choosing what subjects you're going to take in public exams. You are NOT deciding on your future career now. You can always change your mind later and study extra GCSE subjects, but meanwhile, it's good to make informed decisions. Your school will have guidelines to help you make your choices.

My parents really want me to…

Whose choice is it? Are you choosing subjects because they are right for you? Or because they are right for your parents? Or your mates or your teachers? Lots of people will have an opinion. This is your choice.

 Think about:

- ☑ the subjects you are good at.
- ☑ the subjects you enjoy.
- ☑ the subjects you might need for possible careers.
- ☑ a balance of subjects which gives you loads of future possibilities.

"GOOD-ENOUGH" STUFF

- ☑ Are you better at written exams or practical assessments?
- ☑ Are you likely to go on to further study at 16?
- ☑ You may not be able to get your ideal combination of options. What is essential for you?

"I choose a subject and then when I go to the next lesson, I think I don't like it."

Be *honest* about why you're choosing a subject. Try not to make choices based on:

- ☐ whether your friends have chosen a particular subject.
- ☐ who will be teaching you. You may get put in someone else's set!
- ☐ not knowing about a particular subject. Find out! Ask the teachers; look on the web. Ask people further up the school.

"They're not trying to get you to finalise stuff. They're just trying to point you in the right direction."

If you are clear what you want to do but the school is not so happy, talk to your parents or someone you know well, and get them to help you decide what to do next. A teenager recently fought his school because he wanted to be a photographer. The school said he should do more academic stuff. He wrote to all the photo studios near his home and offered to do unpaid work experience for the whole summer. At the end of the summer, they offered him a day-release modern apprenticeship. Four years later, he is a high-profile news photographer in Europe.

UNDER PRESSURE

kinds of different things later on. So unless you're really sure, you may choose not to specialise in one area too early.

"I'm not looking to the future when I choose. If I haven't got the qualifications I need later on, I'll get some more."

"The teachers who like you are really helpful. The ones who don't seem to like you as much can put you down."

What do they mean by "Keep your options open"?

You may be really certain what you want to do with the rest of your life. It's more likely you're not! Keeping your options open means that you take a good combination of subjects so that you could do all

💡 Know that you will always have choices. If you really want to do something, it's never too late to go back and retrain. We have met a few people who have retrained as doctors ten years after leaving school. It's expensive, and it takes years. And they have done it.

Distinguish between learning *skills* and acquiring knowledge. You can get knowledge any time. Skills are what you need in the short term. And some subjects give you loads – even Science and French!

58

"GOOD-ENOUGH" STUFF

Does it matter if you fail?

The important thing is that you give of your best and achieve your potential. That's what really matters.

If you don't do as well as you'd hoped, don't panic. You still have lots of options open to you. There'll always be an opportunity to have another go, if that's what you decide to do. This is not the end!

"If you try your best, it doesn't matter what level you are."

Communication props

"The best way to stop stress before it starts is to communicate."

In order to start relationships and to achieve our goals, we need to communicate. Imagine trying to ask someone to go out with you to the cinema without talking, or using your hands! Maybe if you stared hard enough they might get the message! On the other hand, they might not.

The way we let people know what we think, what we want and what we don't want is by communicating with them. And it's not about how we want to communicate – we need to think of how the person we are speaking to will hear us. It's no good speaking extra-loudly to a French person if they don't understand English and you can't speak French!

59

UNDER PRESSURE

💡 Unless you can communicate well with people, you are going to struggle in many areas of life. *And silence is not a negotiating tool!*

You must learn how to talk to your parents. You also need to learn to communicate with those around you whom you trust. That might be your youth leader, a mature friend, your pastor, an aunt/uncle/grandparent. Whether you find it easy or difficult, you need a team of people around you to whom you can go and let out any frustrations or concerns. If you keep it all to yourself, it will soon damage you. Communication lets it out. It's like the release lever on a pressure valve.

💡 Grunts are also *not* a good communication method. Grunting is OK, but you need to learn to negotiate with your parents. If they say no to something or won't allow you to do something, a huff, grunt or a slammed door will not impress them. They don't know what you're thinking. And if you won't tell them, they'll probably make it up! Ask why they have made that negative decision. Without getting all worked up, say what you feel. And learn to compromise. Try not to attack them: 'You never let me…' Say how you feel. 'I find it really hard when… because…'

🅰️ **…and now for the really helpful bit** Believe it or not, Jesus and his parents had some miscommunication (Luke 2:41–52). Joseph and Mary took 12-year-old Jesus to Jerusalem for the Passover. At the end of the festival, as they were packing up to go home, they thought Jesus was with another part of the group. After a day's travelling, they realised Jesus had been left in Jerusalem and they rushed back. Every mother's nightmare! When they found him in the Temple, they asked him: 'Why have you done this to us?' They were worried. Jesus thought it was obvious where he had been – in his Father's house! But the next few verses are really interesting: Jesus went back to Nazareth and *obeyed* his parents. As far as we know, he never went missing again. He never again assumed that his parents would know where he was.

Being able to communicate is a huge skill which you will need all of your life. With text messaging, email, MSN Messenger and Yahoo Messenger, a lot of communication is done through text language. People can communicate well by text, but find speaking to people a problem. Although technology will give us easy communication over the Internet, we will always have to speak to people face to face.

And finding the right people to talk to can help us become less stressed.

ROUGH STUFF: PRESSURE TO FIT IN

BODY MATTERS

"I'm fed up. I have spots and look awful. And mum won't let me have decent jeans."

So if I buy those trainers, my spots will go and I'll have fab hair?

When you watch an ad on TV, it is not trying to sell you something you need. Advertising experts know that you don't *need* a mobile or a computer or Reebok trainers. They are not essential items in order to be able to live. What they deliberately do is to make you *desire* something. They try and tell you that it is irrelevant whether you need a thing – the issue is whether you desire it. And if you do, then it's OK to buy it. And don't forget – they need you to desire stuff, otherwise their products don't sell.

"I don't care. You wear what you want. I'll wear what I want."

Visually perfect people model every piece of clothing, footwear or cosmetic product in the ads. And they don't have zits! When you watch and desire these items, the issue is not that this jacket will be a good jacket or these jeans will be good jeans but how will this jacket or jeans enhance or even re-create my visual appearance to others? And the standard to reach is that of the person in the TV ad – the fit-looking, well-proportioned, great-complexion model.

> "They think it's cool to wear the same, but I don't want to be in the herd."

What the advertisers want you to feel is that if you look good, then you will feel good, and that, ultimately, life will be good. But the models are airbrushed, and life isn't like that! It's the other way round. If life is good (even if it's up and down), you'll feel good most of the time… and then do you know something? You'll look good. Not necessarily drop-dead gorgeous – some of us never will! But good.

> "It's embarrassing. I had my belly button pierced because everyone else did."

Try watching people. The ones who look good have a calm peacefulness about them. They walk tall. And they have an inner confidence. That's where believing in God can be a great thing: suddenly we know that we're not just some random blob put on the planet to fly solo. We have a purpose.

But I'm too fat

You're between childhood and adulthood, so your body is still changing. A bit of flab doesn't mean that you are too fat. What's important is that what you are taking in as food is roughly what you are expending in energy. So if you sit and watch TV and play on the computer while eating a McDonald's and an ice cream and drinking Coke, maybe it would be a good idea to get a bit more exercise and eat healthier food. Why not walk to school? If you're doing loads of sport and exercise, make sure that you're taking in as much energy as your body needs. Your body isn't ready to diet unless you've been told to do so by a doctor.

 ...and now for the really helpful bit The Bible says that every person on the planet is created in God's image. We reflect something of God in our physical appearance. Now that's awesome. It also means that you look good to God. Is God ugly? No, God's perfect. When God looks at you, it's like looking in a mirror. He sees something of himself in you. Because he created you.

Our bodies change as we grow. Our physical shape changes – our faces change. There is no part of your body that is more than seven years old – your cells, skin and organs are regenerating all the time.

Don't try and look good according to the world's template – your template has been made and God has already said: 'It is good.'

But what about my spots…?

Spots can be a nightmare. Just when you're feeling at your most sensitive, one will always pop up on your nose or your chin. Ouch!

 Around 80 per cent of teenagers suffer with spots, mainly because of hormones. Stress can make them worse. You might get pimples. You might get bad acne. The sebaceous glands in your skin begin to produce too much sebum and begin to block the tiny holes at the base of the fine hairs on your body. And wham! **The holes trap bacteria and the toxins which bacteria produce turn the skin red. Eventually, the walls of the hole get thinner and the spot bursts.**

And don't you want to squeeze them?! Be careful! If there isn't a white head on your spot, and if it's not a blackhead, don't squeeze it. Got that? Don't squeeze a red spot with no head. It's deep inside your skin, and squeezing those spots can cause nasty scars.

Although a good diet can help prevent ordinary spots, acne isn't caused by what you eat or by not washing. It's caused by oil inside the skin. You can buy some helpful products from the pharmacy. If you are seriously concerned about your spots, go and see your doctor.

What are hormones?

People are always saying: 'It's my hormones.' Hormones are accused of being the cause of stress, stroppy mothers, stroppy teens, spots and much more. But what are they?

Hormones are chemicals which are released into the blood stream in one part of the body then travel to another part of the body to do something useful. Amongst other things, they help us grow, manage pain and handle stress.

The two main hormones affecting teenagers are oestrogen and testosterone. The ovaries in girls secrete oestrogen. That starts breast development, pubic hair, widening of the hips and growth spurts.

It's testosterone, created by the testicles, which causes changes in boys. It causes widening of the shoulders, a deeper voice, rapid increase in height and other body changes.

Changing hormones bring perspiration and body odour as well as acne. So if you've grown out of never-washing-until-forcibly-dropped-in-the-shower, but haven't got to

never-leaving-the-shower, now's a good time to stay clean and use antiperspirant or deodorants. Why? Because it's quite stressful enough to have all these changes happen, without having people think you smell!

I've never had dreams like this before! Am I sex mad?

Your body is growing and preparing itself for adulthood. As your hormones change and your body changes, you will begin to feel different and experience different sensations. This includes sex! That's right: your body is now beginning to prepare for when you have sex. God created sex to be something which is good and fun within marriage, as well as being the way to have children. So boys, as you begin to think about girls and dream about them, you could have a wet dream. OK, this may be embarrassing, but it's perfectly natural. Don't worry, and don't get stressed about it. And if you don't want your mum or dad to know about it, learn how to wash the sheets!

For the low-down on relationships check out *Friends First* (see page 95).

It's periods that stress me

Girls, it's your changing hormone levels as you move through puberty which trigger all that! Periods are caused by changing levels of hormones which fluctuate in a regular cycle called the menstrual cycle. This cycle controls fertility and can last anything from 19 to 37 days – 28 days is average. Talk to your mum about it. If you really feel that you can't, make sure you talk to another woman whom you trust. Maybe a friend's mum.

💡 Periods last about five days and can cause stomach cramps in some girls. If you are in agony every month, go and seek advice from your doctor. Meanwhile, there's plenty you can do to reduce the stress. Make sure you have sanitary towels or tampons and a spare pair of knickers at school and if you go away for a sleepover. Especially when you first start your periods, it may take time for a regular cycle to establish itself.

"PERIODS DON'T STRESS ME BUT THEY ARE JUST REALLY ANNOYING."

You might become tired and irritable – even headachy – just before your period. This is called PMS (pre-menstrual syndrome). You might even crave chocolate and stodgy food. Gentle exercise such as swimming, walking or cycling might help this. If it's really bad each month, go to see the doctor.

Mum says I'm moody. So it's all down to hormones, is it?

Maybe. Maybe not! You'll look different as your body changes, and that's hard to handle sometimes. Also, you may feel that you're stuck in the middle. You're not a child… but adults aren't quite ready for you to be an adult, either! This will pass.

💡 If you are feeling low for much of the time, talk to your parents or go to see the doctor. The doctor is there to help you. They won't tell anyone what you've said.

PG, 12A, 15...

"I watch films for entertainment – not because they're a 15 and I'm not. Anyway, films for younger people are only about animals and fairy stories."

Subjecting yourself to subliminal stress...

By the time you're 17, you will have spent an average of 40,000 hours watching films, videos and TV programmes, playing video games, listening to music and reading popular books, but only 11,000 hours in school, 2,000 hours with your parents and 800 hours in church (if you attend regularly).

As a teenager, you have more access to visual images and films through DVDs, videos and the Internet than any generation has had before.

"I think watching 15 or 18 films is OK, but maybe not late at night if I have to go straight to bed."

Around 95 per cent of homes have either a video or DVD player. And there has been such an explosion in videos and in DVDs that trying to stop you watching films is impossible. If your mum says you can't watch *that* film, you simply find somewhere else to watch it. As 52 per cent of teenagers under the age of 16 have a TV in their bedrooms, and 23 per cent have a video as well, it's pretty easy to find somewhere to watch a film!

"It's all part of growing up – you need to start learning about life sometime – so at 12, you could be ready to watch a 15."

ROUGH STUFF

One of the effects of having so much access to the Internet and digital TV is that you are being exposed to more things more quickly. You have access to more information than your parents ever did. This can be a cause of stress, if you are not yet ready to deal with the issues involved.

Just by watching the TV news you can see real life war and violence and even death as it is happening. On the news websites, you can view the dead bodies of terrorists. You may think it's a little strange that adults would let you watch real-life violence, tragedy and death then worry about whether you are watching a 15-certificate film. The trouble is that there is so much violence on our screens, both real and make-believe, that for many of us, it is difficult to distinguish between the two.

 …and now for the really helpful bit The Bible isn't U-certificate, either. Look at Judges 3:21–23, where Ehud sticks a knife into the belly of the king. He was so fat, the Bible says, that the knife handle was covered over with the king's flesh! How about 2 Kings 9:32–36? Jezebel, an evil woman, is thrown out of a window, blood splashing everywhere, and when they came to bury her, only her skull, feet and hands were left. And what about Jesus' crucifixion? It was the most brutal of *all* executions. If the Bible were a film, it would definitely be an 18 certificate!

"PEOPLE TRY TO RUN THROUGH THE WALL AT KINGS CROSS STATION. AND SOME BLOKE WAS KILLED WHEN HE JUMPED ON TOP OF

69

a train and was electrocuted by his eyebrow ring. They only did it because it was in films."

"Yes, I notice the violence and language — but often a 15 is a better story."

Images are very powerful. They affect what you begin to think about and they affect how you feel. The goal of a film is to capture your imagination and your emotions. Why do you get scared when you watch a horror film, or cry if you watch a sad film, or get angry when you see someone who is innocent get hurt in a movie?

Some movie stars who have played bad guys have said that the public shout abuse at them when they walk down a street because they think that's how they are in real life.

For many people, what they see in films and on TV becomes very real to them.

One well-known American TV show about life in the White House, called *The West Wing*, has been so successful that some people actually think that the actor playing the President of the United States was a real President!

Rather than just watching a film anyway, why not discuss it or talk about it?

If you are watching films that are rated too old for you, without your parents knowing, there are several things to think about:

[ ] The film has been given that rating for a reason, no matter

how mature you might be. And you are breaking the law if you are an under-age viewer.

- Who are you going to talk to if something upsets, frightens or disturbs you? When you do something in secret, you often have to cope with the consequences in secret.
- Why have you decided to watch the film? Is it because you really would like to see it, or because your friends are saying you *have* to watch it? Even your parents will choose not to watch some films because they know it will upset them. You need to learn how to make choices for yourself. When you reach 18, will you watch *every* film that's an 18 certificate just because you can? Probably not!
- You are lying to your parents – which is not a godly thing, no matter how unreasonable your parents might appear to be.

...and now for the really helpful bit 'Some of you say, "We can do anything we want to"' says Paul in 1 Corinthians 6:12. 'But I tell you that not everything is good for us. So I refuse to let anything have power over me.' Paul's point is that there are some things you are allowed to do which aren't good for you. People are allowed to smoke, but smoking kills. People are allowed to drink, but too much drink can damage our bodies. People are allowed to eat chocolate bars, but too many can cause you to put on weight.

Life is not just about learning what you are not allowed to do, but also about how to make wise choices.

"I HAD A NIGHTMARE AFTER WATCHING A FILM AND I COULDN'T TELL MY PARENTS

"Because they didn't know I'd watched it."

> It is important to work with your parents and talk through what is appropriate for you, and what isn't. After all, it's not just the films you watch but the images you see and the messages they portray about life and the world you live in today which affect you the most.

All my mates smoke and drink...

But it's cool...
Whatever your mates may say, alcohol, cigarettes and illegal substances are all drugs. And they are all addictive. Having a bit may end up in you finding it difficult to stop. If you smoke 20 cigarettes a day, you will end up spending about £1,400 a year on fags. Imagine what else you could do with the money! And drugs? Although over-the-counter and prescribed drugs can make you well, drug misuse — whether alcohol, tobacco, or illegal drugs — can affect your health.

"My friends are really proud that they smoke."

Plenty of people are proud of doing dumb things. Some people are proud that they steal, others are proud that they got expelled from school. But it seems even sillier to be proud about slowly damaging your body, probably for ever. Your very first cigarette damages airways and lungs and begins to damage blood vessels and cells which are linked to heart attacks and strokes.

⚡ **Despite all the information available about the dangers of smoking, 9 per cent of 11–13 year-olds smoke. If someone gave you a bottle of bleach, which said: '*Danger – do not drink!*' on the bottle, would you drink it? Is it cool to drink bleach? Yet cigarette packets have 'Smoking Kills' on them, in huge letters, and people *still* smoke.**
- **20 per cent of 11–15 year-olds have used illegal drugs.**
- **24 per cent of 11–15 year-olds have drunk alcohol.**

(Statistics from *Young People & Alcohol* by the Institute of Alcohol Studies)

What do I do when I'm offered something?

It can be really difficult to stand up to peer pressure. Wanting to say no and carrying it through are two different things. How can you say no without looking like a dork?

First, you need to *want* to say no. It's natural to be curious, but if you really want to smoke a cigarette, take an illegal drug or drink alcohol, then eventually you will. If you don't want to, just say no firmly. If you are then pushed further, simply walk away. Leave, or ring for someone to pick you up.

💡 **If you think you're in danger of being tempted, try to avoid situations where you know that stuff is going on.**

Stick with friends who agree that they don't want to join in. Together, you can make a difference.

⚡ *You don't have to smoke, or drink, or take drugs.* For instance, statistically, 76 per cent of teens don't drink! It's just not the case that 'everybody's doing it'.

> "PEOPLE WHO SMOKE, TAKE DRUGS OR DRINK NEVER HAVE ANY MONEY."

Remember: addictions cost more than your health – they cost money. Wanting to buy drugs or drink means you need to get the money, and this can mean you lie to, steal from or cheat your parents or others.

> "I DON'T WANT TO TURN INTO THAT KIND OF PERSON."

…and now for the really helpful bit Check out 1 Corinthians 6:19–20. Your body is a house for the Holy Spirit – the Bible calls it a temple. God dwells within you – and your body is a precious thing to him. Jesus died for you. That is why Paul says that God paid a great price for you. So honour God with your body!

GOD STUFF

God stuff:
Pressure as a Christian teen

How do I talk about God with my friends?

"You're talking a lot about God stuff here. My friends think it's rubbish. They keep asking if religion has a place. And I don't know what to say."

People still have stereotypes of Christians sitting in a draughty old church being boring, and your mates may think you're weird if you go to church. They may even tease you about it, which can be stressful.

It's helpful to remember that God stuff isn't actually about religion. It's about a relationship with God which is relevant today and makes a difference to our lives and to the world. Faith makes sense of loads of the nonsense we see around us. And it can change the world.

Does God exist?

⚡ **God exists. You may disagree, but that doesn't mean he doesn't exist!**

75

If you're talking to your mates about your faith, remember: the issue is not usually about whether someone believes in God or not. In fact, most people believe in some power/force/god out there somewhere.

 ...and now for the really helpful bit The Bible doesn't try to prove the existence of God. But it does say that although God is invisible, his power and his character have been plainly visible for everyone to see – in creation (Romans 1:18–20). In other words, just look around you. Look at how creation works, and you have to say there is a designer – God. Many people are likely to agree with you on that one. In fact, Psalm 53:1 says that only a fool would say there is no God (although this is not a verse I would recommend you use with your friends!).

Most people would actually *like* there to be a God. The fact that you are open about your faith may encourage some of your friends to think seriously about Jesus' claims when they are older.

A survey done for the BBC in 2000 (Soul of Britain) said that 70 per cent of people believed in a god of some kind.

If you were to ask people whether they'd want to get to know God and meet him, if they could, the answer would probably be yes. Of course we would like to meet God. The problem is that if people accept that God exists, they have to face a choice:
1. They can ignore the fact that God exists and just live their own life (which is what most non-Christians do).
2. They must radically change how they live.

In fact, 70 per cent of people in the UK think that it's possible God exists, but they are too scared to find out if it's true because of the consequences – a totally different life.

> "LOTS OF PEOPLE THINK SOMETHING PUT THEM HERE ON THIS EARTH. THEY BELIEVE IN FATE. I BELIEVE IN JESUS."

What if they say science proves God doesn't exist?

One basic scientific belief is that something cannot be created from nothing. It sounds very logical and scientific! One of the many arguments which people use against God is: 'OK then, who created God?' or: 'What came before God?' As Christians, we have to say: 'Nothing – God has always existed.' But you can turn the question around and ask: 'OK then, what created the first atom which helped to cause the Big Bang?'

The bottom line is: Do you *want* to believe in an eternal God who created you, loves you and has an exciting life in store for you – or do you prefer to believe in an eternal atom which… does nothing in particular! If you want to believe in God, do some research into Jesus' claims!

So why is right right and wrong wrong?

> "IT'S WHERE OUR MORALS COME FROM."

How do we know what is right and wrong? We all have a conscience. Even those who steal or kill or do bad things know that it is wrong. Our conscience gives us a kick when we have a twinge inside, or a churning stomach, when we tell a lie. Our conscience knows what's right and wrong. We can ignore it but it doesn't go away. Why does our conscience do that? Because our conscience is part of our spirit; our spirit comes from God, and God is just, true and righteous. And when we do things which are against the very character of God, that part of us which is from God tells us so.

"THE TROUBLE WHEN PEOPLE STOP BELIEVING IN GOD IS NOT THAT THEY BELIEVE IN NOTHING, IT IS THAT THEY BELIEVE IN EVERYTHING."
GK Chesterton

...and now for the really helpful bit The Ten Commandments (Exodus 20:1–17) from the Bible are basically the laws for our society today. Christianity does not just have a place in our society – its core values uphold our society.

It's the saddest thing in the world to think that your life is completely meaningless, a result of a mere cosmic freakish accident. It's tragic to think that you live in a world which has pain, disease, death and misery and there is no relief, no answer and no ending to it. And that your struggles and moral choices are meaningless. All you know is that you will one day die and that's it!

THE NUMBER ONE BEST-SELLER

"My mates say the Bible isn't true, and it's just like any book of rules. I think they're wrong, but how do I know?"

So, what's the low-down on the Bible?

The Bible is the world's number one best-selling book – outstripping Harry Potter – and it has been the world's best-seller century after century. It's actually a whole collection of books. The Old Testament covers a huge range of history before Christ was born. The New Testament documents Jesus' life, and the life of the early church. No other book has had such an appeal for so long.

The Bible was never written in one piece – from Genesis to Revelation. None of the people who wrote the different books ever knew that they would end up in one volume. But it's not a collection of unrelated short stories. The Bible has a consistent theme from the beginning to the end. It is the real world, the real-life story of God's plan for everything!

More than 40 authors wrote what we now know as the Bible. Some were kings; others were poor people, fishermen, poets, government officials, teachers or prophets.

The Bible contains historical and archaeological facts, and there is plenty of evidence that events we read of in the Bible really did happen. Have a look on the Internet if you want to find out more.

You can't argue your friends into believing the Bible is true and accurate! The most important thing is reading it yourself, and living your life

with God and the Bible's help. Your friends may well be intrigued – we hope they will!

The Old Testament is full of prophecies – many of which came true with the birth and death of Jesus.

Are there facts not in the Bible which prove it is true?

The Gregorian Calendar, used in many parts of the world today, numbers the years *Anno Domini* – 'In the year of our Lord'. Jesus was born in AD1, give or take a few years, and the significance of his life and death have named the years since.

There are ancient documents which prove Jesus to have been a real person.

The Bible still speaks to people all over the world today. Ask around your church and you will find stories of people whose lives have been changed by what they have read.

"How do I know Christianity is right? Because it's history."

 ...and now for the really helpful bit Paul wrote a letter to his friend Timothy in the first century AD and told him that: 'Everything in the Scriptures is God's Word. All of it is useful for teaching and helping people and for correcting them and showing them how to live.' (2 Timothy 3:16)

I did start reading it and I didn't find it interesting

Maybe the Bible doesn't have the grip of an action-packed film. But it is more relevant than any movie, and it has something to say to you today.

"There's not much entertainment."

ONE UP will help you get into the Bible and hear from God every day! Four easy ways to get hold of **ONE UP**:

1. From your local Christian bookshop
2. Order online at **www.scriptureunion.org.uk**
3. Phone Scripture Union Mail Order direct:
   08450 706 006
4. Take out an annual subscription – contact us for more info!

UNDER PRESSURE

Imagine someone reading you an essay called 'St Mungo's Hospital'. Doesn't sound extra-exciting, does it? Actually, that story is from *Harry Potter and the Order of the Phoenix*. But the excitement and the interest in a series like that comes from the whole plot, the big-picture story. It's not just from a few pages.

"Do you read the Bible?" "Kind of."

Too often we read the Bible by looking at a chapter here and a chapter there, without really understanding what it's about. A real understanding of the whole amazing story of the Bible comes from looking at the whole thing. It shouldn't be about reading page one to the end. It might be by understanding how it all fits together.

"Parables are easy to understand, but the Old Testament is harder."

Bible reading notes are a great way to get into the Bible. So are some of the new translations. *THE MESSAGE* is written in modern language, and is much easier to read than some of the older translations. The story is exactly the same, but it's a more gripping read because it uses language we are more used to. A good novel will grip you while you're reading it. And then it's forgotten. The Bible may change your life for ever.

"I listen to the Bible on a tape."

GOD STUFF

Sometimes I have doubts...

"When I'm on a Christian weekend away or at Soul Survivor, I really feel God's presence. But at home, it never feels the same. I start to doubt, and that really stresses me out."

What do I do if I start having doubts?

"I have doubts when stuff's difficult, and I think: why did this happen?"

First, don't panic! Doubt and uncertainty are normal. And it doesn't mean that you're not a Christian. Weekends away and celebrations are often times when we can feel close to God. Part of that is just being with other people who are wired for God, too. A deeper relationship with Jesus comes from spending time in prayer and reading the Bible on our own, as well as at big events. That might be by talking to God, or by being still and quiet (see Psalm 46:10 – 'Be still, and know that I am God …' (NIV)). Sometimes it's OK, but sometimes it feels like hard work.

> 💡 It's a good idea to find out whether there are youth events in your area. But remember: your relationship with God is based on the quiet stuff, not only on the highs of great music and good company.

You can also look for reminders of God's presence in your everyday world. Look at the sky! Look at nature. As a reminder that God was with them, early Christians looked for the sign of the cross in everything around them – the sail

83

of a boat, a doorway etc. What might you do to remind you that God is involved and active in the world all day, and not just at Christian weekends and when you are praying and reading the Bible?

 ...and now for the really helpful bit Faith is being sure of what we can't see (Hebrews 11:1). Sometimes we can be sure. And sometimes we wonder: 'Why?'

Have a look at the whole of Hebrews chapter 11 and read about all kinds of people who did things with faith, not certainty. Today, when we read their stories, we can see that there's plenty of evidence that God was at work in their lives. But when they were living it, they couldn't see the end of their story. They doubted and were scared sometimes. Just like us!

What are your own stories, and those of friends and family and people in your church, which start: By faith…? It might be helpful to keep a record of them, for times when you're having doubts. For example:
- By faith, Josh went to a new school and made new friends.
- By faith, Dave went to the Gambia on a youth work trip… and people wanted to know more about God after he had told them about Jesus.

You may think these stories are small, but they are significant.

 Many senior scientists believe in God because they say there is no alternative as they look at the complex creation. Although we can't see God, we can see what he has done.

...and now for the really helpful bit We know plenty about Jesus. Paul didn't know Jesus in the flesh, but he says that he knows the one he has faith in (2 Timothy 1:12).

Read the story of 'Doubting Thomas' (John 20:24–29); Jesus helped Thomas overcome his doubts. And you can also ask God to show you himself in different ways. You may not be able to see him face to face in this life, but that's faith.

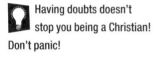 **Having doubts doesn't stop you being a Christian! Don't panic!**

PRAYER PRESSURES

"DOES GOD HEAR ME WHEN I PRAY? I PRAYED THAT I'D DO WELL IN MY EXAMS AND I DIDN'T."

Loads has been written about prayer. That's probably because it's one of the things we find the hardest to do! Everyone struggles with prayer. Even the disciples did – and they were walking and talking with Jesus all the time! That's why they said to Jesus, 'Lord, teach us to pray' (Luke 11:1).

Jesus answered them by teaching them a prayer. Nowadays, it's called the Lord's Prayer. So, when we have the same kind of questions, what better place to start?

UNDER PRESSURE

> "Father, hallowed be your name, your kingdom come. Give us each day our daily bread. Forgive us our sins, for we also forgive everyone who sins against us. And lead us not into temptation."

Luke 11:2–4 (NIV)

- We can call God "Father" because he loves us like a perfect dad
- "hallowed" means "holy"
- in God's kingdom, everything is good, right and just
- "sin" means "things we do wrong"
- "temptation" is when we want to do something we know isn't good!

Does this mean we can pray for loads of money, or for God to blow up people we don't like? Or can we pray to pass our exams when we haven't done any work? No.

"We don't always get what we want."

We can't pray for anything we want. Well, we can, but God won't always say yes.

"Prayer doesn't work sometimes."

It's easy to fall into the trap of thinking that we need to get God's attention. We need to jump up and down and wave so that he might just notice us. After all, we think we are competing with billions of other people for God's attention. Is that right?

Imagine being at a concert and your favourite singer comes on. Imagine, in the midst of thousands of people, they stop and search the crowd. They see you there, smile, point at you and say your name. How would you feel? Incredible! That's exactly what happens with God. He looks for you. You don't need to go to try and find him or get his attention.

"God does always answer. But we may not get what we expect."

 …and now for the really helpful bit A couple of the disciples were angry at how Jesus was being treated in one place they visited (Luke 9:52–56). So they asked Jesus if they should call down (pray for) fire from heaven to destroy the village. Jesus' response? He told them off.

But here is the amazing thing. If we pray like Jesus taught us, we're definitely asking God for the right kinds of things. And we can trust him to help us and to give us what we need.

UNDER PRESSURE

⚡ Sometimes we can feel pressure to pray. But actually that's pressure to talk to someone we love. Look at it another way, as an opportunity to talk to our Father God. We can offload our worries and tell him what we're scared about. Life's complicated. It can stress us out. Prayer isn't a duty. God isn't angry when we don't pray. Prayer is a pleasure – God is saying: 'You can talk to me. I can help you.'

💡 Prayer is the *ultimate* stress-reliever. Don't let the devil deceive you into thinking it's stressful!

Disliking people

"I can't stand this boy in my church. I know it says in the Bible we should love our neighbour. But I can't."

There will always be some people we like. And some we don't. You can't be best mates with everyone. Some people may irritate you because of what they wear or how they speak – or don't speak! They may remind you of someone else you don't like very much. It's a tough thing to say, but if it's any of these, get over it! We can't be clones. And variety is a good thing. Get to know them a bit. If you don't like someone because they're geeky and irritating, that's wrong. *You'll* have to change.

GOD STUFF

 ...and now for the really helpful bit Jesus talked a lot about love. In fact, loving others is one of the key things which people notice in Christians. He gave us a new command: 'You must love each other, just as I have loved you. If you love each other, everyone will know that you are my disciples.' (John 13:34–35) It shows. Someone doesn't have to be your best mate for you to love them. Openness, friendliness and kindness are all great signs of love.

And the definition of love? Look at 1 Corinthians 13. And check out *Friends First* for more love stuff! (See page 95.)

She hurt my feelings!

OK, it may be that she has done something or said something to you which was wrong. But by choosing to feel so cross about it, you are also damaging yourself. Comes back to choice again!

 ...and now for the really helpful bit So what could you do?

- ✅ Pray about it then just get on with life (sounds simple but it can work).
- ✅ Jesus told his followers that if it needs more than that, just to go and try and sort it out (Matthew 5:21–26).
- ✅ Jesus then told his followers that if even that doesn't work, take someone along and sort it out together (Matthew 18:15–17).
- ✅ **And if it's still a problem, and the person isn't listening, walk away. You have done all you can.**

If, on the other hand, the disagreement was your fault, then you will need to apologise and ask for forgiveness. It might take time, and you might need someone to help you sort it out. The great news is that Jesus tells us he will forgive us! But sometimes it takes human beings a bit longer.

Finally... see if you can say the prayer which Jesus taught his disciples — without a feeling in your guts: Forgive us our sins as we forgive those who sin against us. If that's still stressing you, find someone to talk to who will help you see where to go next.

> Remember: you can't change others; you can only change yourself (or even better, ask God to do it!).

CHECKLIST
- Why do I dislike this person?
- What can I do?
- What should I pray?
- Am I being unreasonable/unfair?

My friend says those people in the church down the road aren't Christians

How d'you know if it's a cult?
There are lots and lots of different churches all over the world who follow Jesus Christ. There are also some that don't share exactly the same beliefs as ours. It can be confusing. So which ones are OK?

As Christians, we have to juggle our place in God's world and his plan. The bottom line is that we believe that Jesus Christ is the Son of God. And we believe that we have:
1. authority from God (the Bible).
2. experience of God within us (the Holy Spirit).
3. a sense of belonging and fellowship (the church).
4. an outline for practical living (in the Bible).

Christianity has these in balance, but cults sometimes focus on one point much more heavily, or on the personality of a leader. At the fringe of the Christian church, some of the edges are fuzzy, and it is difficult to be clear whether a group is Christian or a cult. Good questions to ask are: whose authority is dominant in this group – the Bible's or the leader's? Are the people free? Because in 2 Corinthians 3:17 it says: 'The Lord and the Spirit are one and the same, and the Lord's Spirit sets us free.'

The same criteria work for other mainstream faiths such as Islam. The balance between the four areas is there, although the focus on Jesus is not. Like Christianity, Islam has cults which have a heavy focus on one area.

So even if they believe similar things to Christian groups, cults actually control people – and that's the difference.

If you have a hunch that something is a little cultish, look at the above four areas, pray, reflect and bounce your thoughts around with your mates or an older Christian who isn't involved with the church you're concerned about!

I don't understand what the deal is with the different denominations

The difference between churches or denominations that follow Jesus is a bit like the difference between football teams. All football supporters like football. They even worship it, sometimes! But some like Man U; others like REAL Madrid, and some like a Sunday afternoon kick around at the park. It's all football. There are hundreds of places to watch or play football. Likewise, there are many different kinds of churches. Some are loud and noisy, with loads of music. Some are very quiet. Some have liturgy (using prayer books). Others only have a PowerPoint projector!

What's important is that you find a church where you can get something. And give something.

WHAT ABOUT OTHER RELIGIONS?

"Some of my friends have different religions. How do I know that Christianity is the right one?"

That's a good question, and it's not easy to give a one-sentence answer. I have heard Christians say to Muslims, Buddhists or Jews that Christianity is the only way to heaven. For many people, that is an outrageously arrogant claim and it upsets them. It is also false. Christianity is not the only way to God.

The only way to God is through Jesus. OK, that's still an arrogant statement for a Christian to make. The point is that Christians don't make that statement; the Bible does. Or, more accurately, Jesus himself says: 'I am the way, the truth, and the life! Without me, no one can go to the Father.' (John 14:6) This is a very definite statement. No room for discussion or other possibilities. Jesus is the way, the truth and the life.

It's not about whether Christianity is the true religion or about what Christians have done wrong or right over the last 2,000 years. Christians have done great things: they led the fight to abolish the slave trade, and set up companies (such as Cadbury's, yum!) which gave their workers better rights. However, stuff has been done in the name of Christianity which now seems inhumane: armies were sent on 'Crusades' to the Middle East to take back Jerusalem; soldiers murdered women and children in the name of Jesus Christ; even today – over 700 years later – Muslims talk about what the Christians did to their ancestors. In other centuries, Christians owned people as slaves, or burned alive those with different religious views.

> **The question isn't about religion or culture. The question for you and me is: WHAT DO WE THINK ABOUT JESUS?**

There are two things about Christianity which make it very different from other religions:
- It's historically accurate. Abraham was a real person, King David a real king. Jesus was a real man. The true history of Israel is the true history of the Bible. So the Bible isn't a set of philosophical statements or good ideas, but an account of how God has dealt with a group of people throughout history.
- The claims of Jesus. Jesus said he was God: 'I am one with the Father'. (John 10:30) If Jesus is God, the Creator of the universe, then it would be wise to listen to what he has to say.

So the claims of Christianity all hinge on Jesus, who he was and what happened to him.

> **…and now for the really helpful bit** Jesus was once at a meeting when a group of friends lowered from the roof a paralysed man (Luke 5:18–26). Jesus looked at the man and said to him, 'Your sins are forgiven.' Now, the religious leaders who were there were shocked. Why? Because they believed two things: first, that if you were ill or paralysed, it was because God was punishing your sins. Secondly, they believed that only God could change that situation. Jesus knew this, which is why he asked them the question: 'Is it easier for me to tell this crippled man that his sins are forgiven or to tell him to get up and walk?' When Jesus made the man walk, the only explanation was that God was at work. So what Jesus said in the

first place – that the man's sins were forgiven – was true. The man's sins were forgiven, and he could now walk.

It's not about a battle between Christianity, Islam, Hinduism or Buddhism, or any other religion. Jesus made some very specific and direct claims, and he did some very specific and direct things. There is nothing more incredible than being killed, only to rise from the dead!

 …and now for the really helpful bit If Jesus Christ did not rise from the dead, then Christianity is an absolute waste of my time and yours. It even says that in the Bible (see 1 Corinthians 15:16–17). So, did Jesus rise from the dead? Well, first, the religious leaders knew that if he had, then he was undoubtedly God. Only God could defeat death. If they wanted to discredit Jesus, all they had to do was to produce a body. Some people say that the disciples stole the body. Well, it's hard enough today (apparently) to get rid of a human body but 2,000 years ago – with no car, no electric saws, in a heat where a body would stink within hours – where would you hide the body? How would you keep people from discovering it? It was illegal to steal a body. In fact, it was punishable by death. Would you have risked stealing a body when Roman soldiers guarded it?

For Christians, the ultimate proof that Jesus rose from the dead is that you can meet him today, one on one. It's impossible to have a relationship with a dead person!

If you have friends who belong to other religions you *must* respect their beliefs as they are very important to them. Disagreeing and being rude aren't the same thing!

Look out for
Friends First

by Claire Pedrick
and Andy Morgan!

"All Christian blokes are wet! I don't fancy any of them!"

"My mates are all going out with someone. What's so wrong with me?"

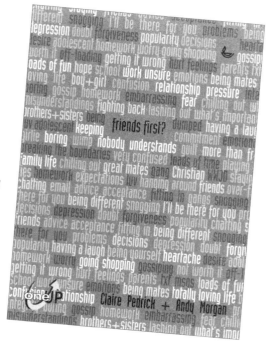

Sound familiar? This book takes a look at relationships and how confusing they can get; friendship groups, girlfriends, best friends, boyfriends and even being friends with your parents!

Friends First will help you untangle some of these relationships for yourself.

ISBN 1 85999 644 2

You can buy this book at your local Christian bookshop, or online at
www.scriptureunion.org.uk/publishing or call Mail Order direct: **08450 706 006**

index

Alcohol 10, 72, 73
Bedtime 46
Careers 53, 55-56
Change 4-5, 11-12, 14-15, 18-19, 53, 55, 64-67, 75-76, 80, 82, 88, 90, 93
Communication 4-6, 59-61
Cults 90-91
Death 11, 21-23, 69, 78, 80, 94
Decisions 5-6, 23, 50, 56
Diet 64-65
Disliking people 88-90
Divorce 11, 16-20
Doubt 83-85
Drugs 10, 45, 72-74
Environment 29-31
Exams 4, 11, 32-34, 38-39, 45, 47, 56-57, 85, 87
Failure 33-34, 58-59
Forgiveness 18, 89
Healthy eating 10, 64

Homework/school work 6, 9, 32-38, 41, 43, 45, 48, 52-53, 87
Hormones 11, 64-67
Money 6, 45, 49-52, 54, 72, 74, 87
News 26-28, 69
Options 41, 43, 56-59
Other religions 92-94
Parents 8, 11, 14, 16-21, 23-24, 27-28, 34, 37-38, 43-49, 52, 56-57, 60-61, 67, 69-72, 74
note to parents 4-7
Periods 8, 66-67
Prayer 10, 25, 32, 39, 42, 83, 85-88, 90-91
Pressure 4, 6, 8-11, 26-27, 32-33, 38-45, 47-49, 51, 53, 56, 60, 62, 73, 75, 85, 88
from parents 8, 18, 38, 43-47, 56
to be like your brother or sister 47-48

to be perfect 19, 62, 64
Relaxing 33, 35, 39
Safety 27, 42, 45
SATS 38, 41
School 4-5, 7, 11-12, 14-15, 32-38, 41, 47, 53, 56-57, 68
Smoking 71-74
Spots 62, 64-65
Stress 4-5, 8-11, 14, 19, 27, 36-40, 43, 53, 55, 59, 61, 64-69, 75, 83, 88, 90
prevention 4, 10-11, 27, 36-39, 55, 61, 65-67, 88, 90
Suffering 22, 24-25
Temptation 73, 86
Terrorism 26
War 11, 26-27, 69
Work 7, 33, 50, 52-55, 57
Worries 8, 17, 29, 88